Sharon L. Sage

rom: Beth Sage Emsun, Christmas 1990

QUILT

MASTERPIECES

QUILT
MASTERPIECES

by Susanna Pfeffer

PARK LANE

NEW YORK

This 1990 edition published by PARK LANE,

Distributed by Outlet Book Company, Inc.,
a Random House Company, 225 Park Avenue South
New York, New York, 10003

Printed and bound in Hong Kong
ISBN 0-517-03297X

© 1988 Hugh Lauter Levin Associates, Inc.
Photo research: Dennis Duke

9 8 7 6 5 4 3 2 1

QUILT MASTERPIECES

A QUILT IS A TEXTILE LAYER CAKE OR SANDWICH: two pieces of fabric with a filling between the layers. The upper layer, or top, as the most visible, is decorative. The bottom layer, or backing, is utilitarian. The filling, known as batting, provides warmth and loft, or thickness. *Quilting* is the term used for the stitches, usually decorative, that hold the three layers together, keep the filling from shifting, and help trap air, which acts as an insulator.

HISTORY

No one knows who first discovered that two pieces of cloth, stuffed with something soft and held together with stitching, would provide cozy protection from the cold. But the news—and the technique—spread quickly. Long before decorative quilting appeared in Europe, the people of China, India, Egypt, Persia, and Turkestan were using padded fabrics for clothing, bedding, and even armor. The ancient Romans had quilted mattresses, bedcovers, and cushions, and their soldiers probably protected themselves with arrow-resistant body coverings. The Crusaders first encountered this type of garment on the bodies of their enemies, the Saracens, and from the eleventh century, soldiers all over the world wore quilted shirts and coats for both warmth and protection. In our century, the wearing of protective padded garments survives in the use of the bulletproof vests worn by some law enforcement personnel. Fortunately, the vast majority of quilted fabrics are now employed in completely benign ways.

Somewhere between the thirteenth and fifteenth centuries, the art of quilting for beauty as well as utility grew up in Europe. In Italy, a form of quilting known as trapunto was developed. This technique, which is still used today, requires two layers of fabric but no batting. A design is outlined with running stitches, and the area within the stitching is then stuffed from the back to raise it from the background. By the seventeenth century, quilting as we know it—along with the related crafts of patchwork and appliqué—was to be found on all kinds of clothing, both outer wear and undergarments, as well as on bedspreads.

With the arrival of Dutch and English settlers in the New World, quilting took on a new life and flourished; during the late-eighteenth and nineteenth centuries, it became America's premier folk art. The earliest settlers, in need of warm bedcovers, had little to work with in the way of materials, so they carefully hoarded every scrap of fabric and usable portion of worn garments. Since even small cloth remnants could be used in patchwork quilts, they became the most prevalent type at this time. A patchwork quilt was thus a souvenir or record of a family's history, incorporating bits of garments and other household textiles. Although quiltmaking was primarily a useful art, its practitioners turned necessity into social occasions—quilting parties and quilting bees—where the women would work together to finish a quilt while the men and children feasted and played games. During this period, quilters developed a multitude of patchwork patterns that, because of their great popularity, became part of the folk tradition. These patterns bear the most picturesque names, among them Log Cabin, Flying Geese, Drunkard's Path, Kansas Troubles, Grandmother's Flower Garden, Lone Star, Bear's Paw, Broken Dishes, and Windmill. (The names of identical patterns often differ from region to region.)

As the frontier was conquered and made safe for the settlers, living conditions improved and, with prosperity and the availability of more materials, quilts became less austere. Patchwork quilts were more likely to be made of new and finer fabrics, and appliqué quilts, which require more fabric, began to emerge. These, too, developed a body of traditional patterns. Fancy quilts came out of the bedroom to become part of the living room decor. By the early twentieth century, fewer quilts were made out of strict need, and more and more were made to satisfy a creative urge. Today, many regard quilting as being in the same league with painting and sculpture; like its fellow arts, it is still evolving.

TYPES OF QUILTS

Quilts can be classified according to the materials from which they are made, the techniques used to create or embellish them, their cultural or geographical origin, the uses to which they are put, or their chronological position. These categories are not necessarily clear-cut or exclusive; two or more may overlap, as we shall see. What follows is a brief description of the most common American quilt categories.

Pieced or Patchwork

Any quilt top whose design is composed of separate elements seamed together can be classified as pieced. In patchwork, either new fabric or carefully saved scraps are cut into pieces and set together to form designs. The pieces, or patches, are usually simple geometric shapes: squares, triangles, diamonds, rectangles, hexagons, and circles. The patches, which must be precisely cut in order for the edges to fit each other exactly, are often assembled into easily handled units called blocks. The blocks are sewn together into strips, then the strips are joined to form the completed quilt top. Sometimes a border is added.

A variant of the patchwork quilt is the Postage Stamp quilt. The term implies miniaturization, a correct conclusion. However, it is the pieces making up the design that are small, not the quilt itself. Any patchwork pattern, traditional or otherwise, can be reduced to postage stamp proportions, but accuracy in cutting and stitching becomes even

more crucial, and a great deal of painstaking work is involved. The results, however, can be quite spectacular.

The sampler quilt, too, is usually a patchwork type. Just as Colonial samplers of the eighteenth and early nineteenth centuries were a compendium of as many different embroidery stitches as possible, so a sampler quilt contains numerous patchwork patterns.

Appliqué

The French word *appliqué* means *applied*, and it is used to denote both the technique and the decorative pieces used in it. In ancient times, appliqués may have been used to cover worn spots. For a quilt, appliqué motifs are cut from one or more fabrics and are laid on top of a background, a larger piece of another fabric. The edges of the appliqué are carefully turned under to prevent fraying; they are then sewn to the background, usually by hand, using tiny, invisible slip stitches. Since appliqué quilts require more fabric than patchwork quilts, they are usually associated with more affluent times. The designs range from simple stylized floral or animal shapes to elaborate pictorial motifs.

Embroidered

Sometimes the major decorative element of a quilt top is embroidery; the Rainbow Monogram and Initial quilt by Ida W. Beck, pictured on page 43, is a superb instance. More commonly, however, embroidery plays a secondary, though still important, role in embellishing a patchwork, appliqué, or crazy quilt. The latter two types in particular often benefit from the addition of embroidery to create details too small or intricate to be accomplished by other means. In crazy quilts, the edges of the patches are frequently overlaid with embroidery. Cotton, silk, rayon, linen, and wool embroidery threads may be used, along with every conceivable embroidery stitch.

Crazy

The crazy quilt is a unique type of patchwork that reached the height of its popularity in the Victorian era. Instead of geometric patches arranged in an established pattern, irregularly shaped scraps are pieced together, usually into blocks that are later joined; these, too, are often irregular in shape and size. The favorite materials for crazy-quilt patchwork are silks, velvets, brocades, satins, and taffetas —either new or salvaged from worn-out garments and home furnishings. The most typical examples of crazy quilts are lavishly embroidered. The edges of the patches are covered, generally with feather stitching, to hide the raw edges; additional embroidered decorations are then worked on the patches.

Album

Album quilts came into their full flowering in the years just before and after 1850 in Baltimore, Maryland. These quilts were assembled from a series of appliquéd pictorial blocks, each one resembling a page of an album. On some quilts, the floral, his-

8

torical, or scenic motifs were cut from preprinted fabrics; on others, the appliquéd designs were created entirely from shapes cut from solid and print fabrics. The blocks, with embroidery frequently added to improve the detail, were joined together; sometimes strips of a contrasting color, known as sashing, were inserted between the blocks. Often several individuals pooled their talents to make a quilt, each one signing her own block and thereby contributing to the album spirit.

Closely allied to the album quilt is the friendship, or presentation, quilt. This type also consists of blocks, each one worked and signed by a different person. Designs and techniques may be uniform or vary according to the whims of the makers. Such a quilt is usually presented to an individual as a gift, or it may be displayed by an organization.

Commemorative, Patriotic, and Political

In the nineteenth century especially, all kinds of textiles were manufactured to highlight important events, such as presidential elections and centennial celebrations. Printed ribbons, handkerchiefs, bandannas, and the like were collected, sewn together in various ways, and turned into quilts. Lacking commercial textiles, quilters created their own commemorative quilts using patchwork, appliqué, embroidery, and other techniques to honor their country, a historical event, prominent individuals, relatives, or friends. One of the most striking and bizarre examples is Elizabeth Roseberry Mitchell's Graveyard quilt, page 71, which she cre-

ated in memory of her deceased children and other relatives.

Amish/Mennonite

The Amish were a breakaway sect of the Mennonites, who were persecuted in Europe for their strict religious beliefs. They began migrating to this country in the early eighteenth century, settling mostly in Pennsylvania and the Midwest. To the present day, the Amish continue to adhere to their practices, holding their worship services at home rather than in a church, prohibiting the use of electricity and automobiles, and avoiding higher education. Further religious splits occurred, the main one being the division between the strict Old Order Amish and the more liberal Mennonites, who worship in church and accept modern technology.

Because quilts were considered utilitarian, making them was allowed, offering women an opportunity to socialize as well as to be creative. Although the Amish are not permitted to wear bright colors, their quilts are by no means so restricted, and many beautiful Amish quilts contain colors we would consider quite exotic. Pennsylvania Amish quilts are usually made of wool and are pieced together using squares, triangles, diamonds, and rectangles, often quite large and few in number. The quilting stitches tend to be simple but decorative. A good Amish quilt in a typical pattern—such as Diamond in a Square, Bars, or Nine-Patch—is highly prized today. Midwestern Amish and Mennonite quilts are more commonly made of cotton, and their patterns and colors are often more conventional than those of their Pennsylvania cousins.

Hawaiian

The Hawaiian quilt is a unique phenomenon, influenced both by native folk craft and design and by the influx of European and American settlers. Early Hawaiian textiles were made from a paperlike fabric produced from the bark of trees. They were painted or stamped with motifs based on native trees, shrubs, flowers, and produce. After the islanders learned the Western technique of quilting, the same motifs found their way into native quilts. The designs would usually take the form of a single large, stylized appliqué, cut freehand from a large piece of cloth folded into quarters or eighths. The unfolded appliqué was placed in the center of the quilt; a complementary border, cut from the same fabric, would complete the design. The quilting stitches followed the outline of the appliquéd shapes, giving a puffy, undulating quality to the work—reminiscent, some say, of ocean waves. Another popular theme found in many Hawaiian quilts is the national flag; a quilt of this type might be a combination of piecing and appliqué techniques, with geometric quilting.

Contemporary

The designation *contemporary* is both chronological-historical and stylistic, since a contemporary quilt can be executed in any technique or pattern. Many contemporary quilts are simply re-creations of traditional patterns a century or more old; the only

10

difference is in the use of new materials and the probable use of a sewing machine for part or all of the work. Conversely, old quilts exist that, because of their color or design or some other factor, have a decidedly modern feeling. A case in point is the Broken Star, or Carpenter's Wheel, quilt on page 17; it is over 100 years old, but it looks as though it could have been made yesterday. Some new quilts could be considered reinterpretations or adaptations of old designs, reflecting tradition, but with a new twist. Jinny Beyer's Ray of Light quilt (page 101) would fall into that category. But we are most likely to use the term *contemporary* to characterize works that are abstract, futuristic, expressionistic, evolutionary, or innovative—or, perhaps, difficult to classify in any other way.

MATERIALS

The quilt top and backing may be cotton—by far the most common material—or a cotton/synthetic blend, wool, silk, satin, velvet, or almost any combination of these. It is customary, but not mandatory, to back the quilt with the same kind of fabric used for the top.

The batting is a sheet of loosely compressed—not woven—fibers of wool, cotton, or polyester. Before commercially manufactured batting became available, quilters used whatever came to hand: uncarded cotton, sheared wool, feathers, old blankets, etc. Since the nineteenth century, however, they could purchase batting for their quilts. Cotton was the most popular material and is still used today. However, more and more quilters prefer polyester batting because it is lightweight, launders easily, and—since it doesn't shift as much as cotton—requires fewer and less closely spaced quilting stitches.

Quilting thread is made especially for the purpose. The most favored kind is mercerized cotton, which is glazed or waxed for extra strength and luster.

HOW A QUILT IS CONSTRUCTED

Regardless of the technique used to create the top, almost all quilts are assembled in the same manner. Once the top is completed, the edges are trimmed, if necessary, to correct any irregularities. The backing fabric, pieced as needed, is usually cut the same size as the top. But sometimes the backing is intended to finish the edges, too. In this case, it is cut a little larger than the top to allow for turning it to the top side and enclosing the edges like a binding. The backing fabric is placed face down on a large, flat surface. The batting is placed over the backing and trimmed to the same size. Then the top is carefully centered and positioned face up over the batting and the layers smoothed out to eliminate any creases or lumps. Using large straight or safety pins, the three layers are fastened at intervals of a few inches, starting at the center. Then, starting at the center, the layers are basted together (sewn by hand with long running stitches) lengthwise, crosswise, and diagonally. More rows of basting are then added to keep the layers from shifting.

At this point, the quilting design can be marked on the quilt top. There are numerous designs available to the quilter. Among the simplest are parallel rows, either vertical, horizontal, or diagonal. Crossing these with perpendicular rows produces square, box, or diamond quilting. Some of the more popular fancy quilting stitches are scroll, chain, plume, and rose wreath—each with many variations. Quilting can also follow the outline of appliquéd shapes; this is known as outline, contour, or echo quilting.

The quilt is now fastened to a quilting frame, a wooden support on legs that stretches the layered fabrics and keeps them taut. A large embroidery hoop on a stand can also be used, but it does not allow a large area to be worked on at one time. When a large frame is used, two or more people can sit around it and work the quilting, which is done by hand using a short, sharp needle and strong, glazed quilting thread. Once the exposed area is quilted, it is unfastened and a new section is moved into place for quilting. After the quilting is done, the piece is removed from the frame, and the edges are finished, either with a separate bias binding or by bringing the backing around to the top side as a self-binding.

QUILTS IN OUR LIVES

We have already seen how quilting evolved from an ancient, strictly utilitarian technique to a highly sophisticated art form. Whereas quilted fabrics once served mainly to keep the body warm and protect it from injury, they now grace our homes, hang on gallery walls, and illuminate centuries of history. We have seen how our ancestors—European and especially American—nurtured the crafts of patchwork, appliqué, and quilting into a folk art that today is esteemed over the entire world, an art that continues to develop in new directions.

Of course, there is something special about snuggling under a warm quilt on a cold night. Though light in weight, the quilt soon traps the body's heat in the air cells created by its unique combination of layering and stitching and becomes a cozy, enveloping shield that no icy blast can penetrate. But a quilt is more than just a warm covering, as countless people have discovered: Professional decorators, magazine editors, and imaginative homedwellers alike are using quilts in new or rediscovered ways. Though often associated with country living, quilts are just as welcome and aesthetic in a town house or city apartment. Apart from their practical and decorative use as bedcovers, quilts can be used as tablecloths, as covers or throws on a sofa or chair, as curtains, or as wall hangings.

Collecting quilts has become a popular—if increasingly expensive—hobby, and collectors have found all sorts of ways to use and display their quilts. Sometimes an old quilt, too damaged to use as a whole, has intact sections that can be cut out and made into throw pillows, stuffed toys, or pincushions. These can be a charming adjunct to almost any decorating scheme, and they also make wonderful gifts. Naturally, a fine antique quilt in good condition would be treasured by anyone fortunate enough to receive one as a gift. Properly cared for, such a piece will become a cherished heirloom while appreciating in value. The same can be said for the best works of our outstanding contemporary quilters. Anyone interested in this aspect of quilting can become acquainted with antique quilts, as well as the work of contemporary artists, through antique shows, museum exhibitions, and books, newsletters, and other specialized publications.

QUILT MASTERPIECES

In this volume, quilts are presented by type, although you must bear in mind that many are composites of two or more types and could fall into more than one category. For the most part, the quilts are then arranged historically within each grouping, although thematic and aesthetic progression or the need for variety may occasionally take precedence over strict chronology. Each photograph is accompanied by a descriptive text, headed by the title of the quilt, the name of its creator (if known), the material and technique used, the size, the date, the place of origin (if known), and its present ownership.

QUILT
MASTERPIECES

1

BROKEN STAR OR CARPENTER'S WHEEL
Pieced cotton. 80×80".
c. 1880. Illinois.
General Foods Corporate Collection.

The first viewing of this quilt's bold design, which consists of a few large pieces in sharply contrasting colors, might lead one to think it is a contemporary quilt. Actually, it is over 100 years old.

To create a patchwork quilt, the maker would typically assemble small patches into a series of blocks of the desired pattern; she would then join the blocks to form the quilt top. Here, however, a single block—in this case, the Broken Star, or Carpenter's Wheel, motif—has been enlarged to almost heroic proportions with great effectiveness. The elements of the design are pure and simple: three geometric shapes—a square, a triangle, and a diamond; and three print fabrics —a dark fabric, a bright one, and a light one. The bright and dark fabrics are then repeated in a wide double border.

The quilting design is simple, too. On the squares and diamonds, the stitching is done in parallel rows; on the triangles, the stitching turns the corner at the apex of the triangle. The borders are quilted in a scalloped-chain (braid) motif. The entire quilt is beautifully planned and executed. It is an imaginative and sophisticated example of quiltmaking whose appeal has not diminished with age.

2 Log Cabin (Barn Raising, or Sunshine and Shadow Variation)

Pieced cotton. 80½×64¼″.
c. 1890. Kentucky.
Collection The Kentucky Historical Society, Frankfort.

No collection of American quilts could be considered comprehensive without the inclusion of one or two examples of the log cabin pattern. A classic instance of this very widely used motif is the one shown here. The basic log cabin block is extremely simple. It starts with a small square. A narrow strip, equal in length to the side of the square, is joined to one edge, forming a rectangle. The next strip—equal in width to the preceding one but longer—is joined to one long edge of the rectangle. Succeeding strips, always the same width but progressively longer as needed, are joined to each newly created edge, around and around, until a square block of the desired size is achieved.

Variations are obtained through the use of color and the way the blocks are set together. In this quilt, each block is pieced so as to divide it in half diagonally, with bright colors on one side and black on the other. The blocks are then arranged to create the series of concentric, strongly contrasting bands known as Barn Raising. The alternate name, Sunshine and Shadow, is a reference to an Amish pattern that is usually worked in squares rather than strips, which produces a similar interplay of dark and light. Many other log cabin variations are possible, merely by shifting the position of the dark sides of the blocks. These include Windmills, Lightning, and Furrows (the Straight Furrow variation is shown on page 21).

One unique feature of this particular quilt is the spectacular red-and-black starburst in the center. The blocks that form it are assembled just like all the others, except that red and black are used exclusively. Notice, too, that there are several shades of black throughout the quilt—a result, no doubt, of piecemeal fabric collecting over a period of years.

3 Log Cabin

Pieced silk and satin. 67½×58½".
c. 1890. New Jersey.
The Shelburne Museum, Shelburne, Vermont;
gift of Mrs. Carl Johnson, Bogota, New Jersey.

This beautiful Log Cabin quilt owes its special elegance and luxury to the silk and satin fabrics from which it is made. Most Log Cabins are made of cotton or wool, which provide sturdiness and serviceability along with the appeal of the design. The quilt pictured here, however, has a certain delicacy and refinement that are equally appealing. The individual blocks are constructed exactly like those of the example shown on page 19. The only difference is that, instead of the solid black used for half of the block, two or more dark colors are alternated. In contrast to this rather severe arrangement, the colored half of each block contains several brighter prints and solids, which, though somewhat freer in concept, are still controlled enough to create a definite degree of shading. Note, too, that every block starts with a small red square. By arranging the dark half of each block in the same position —here, toward the lower left—the quilter has created a variation known as Straight Furrow. Thanks to the careful planning and placement of colors, there is a constant shift from dark to light as the viewer's eye is drawn up along the path of the furrows.

A final luxurious touch is the wide border used to finish the edges. With its subtle, unobtrusive tone-on-tone floral print and perfect proportions, it is just the right frame for the log cabin design.

4

HEXAGONS AND TRIANGLES
Pieced cotton. 97×76″. 1850s. Place of origin unknown.
The Shelburne Museum, Shelburne, Vermont;
gift of Electra Havemeyer Webb.

This remarkable quilt, dating from the mid-nineteenth century, foreshadows a twentieth-century phenomenon: the skeletal framework of the geodesic dome, which is based on interlinked hexagonal members. Its creator, of course, was not aware of this connection, yet it is both stimulating and sobering to reflect that concepts that we view as contemporary or even futuristic may have their roots in earlier, less-sophisticated times.

What we see here is an illusion of shapes laid over other shapes: The golden-yellow spokes and the bright red hubs appear to stand out sharply against the background, a green-and-brown ombré print. In fact, the arrangement is pieced together rather than applied in layers. The apparent background consists of triangles; the spokes are rectangular strips; and the hubs are hexagons. At the top and bottom of the hub-and-spoke field are double borders of red and yellow.

Also unusual is the outer border of the quilt. The top and bottom are bounded by a simple strip of the background fabric. The sides, however, are edged in a repeating diamond-in-a-rectangle motif (actually diamonds joined to triangles), with the motifs alternating in color. Even the binding around the edges varies, with yellow along the top and bottom and red along the sides.

The quilting, too, is just a bit out of the ordinary. Whereas the yellow spokes are stitched lengthwise in parallel rows, the intervening triangles are worked variously in parallel, triangular, or pyramidal rows. And on the red hubs, the hexagonal stitching is worked in a continuous spiral rather than in separate, concentric units. Finally, the top and bottom borders are diagonally quilted, while the side borders are contour-quilted around the pieced shapes.

5 STAR

Pieced cotton, silk, velvet, and linen. 65×66".
c. 1890. New York.
The Shelburne Museum, Shelburne, Vermont;
gift of Mr. and Mrs. Peter Paine, New York City.

Reflecting the comforts of urban prosperity, this quilt is as far removed as possible from the scrimp-and-save thrift imposed on pioneers. By the late nineteenth century, the availability of many fine fabrics, at least for those who had the money, made it unnecessary to raid the scrap bag in order to create a quilt. Indeed, in many homes, quilts were considered part of the decor instead of a mere means of providing warmth. It is very likely that the example pictured here, assembled from deliberately selected fine fabrics, was tossed with careless yet artful grace over a sofa in a Victorian parlor.

The quilt comprises 25 blocks in a variant of the pieced-star pattern, a motif made up entirely of triangles. The blocks are identical except for the color arrangement. Whether the eight-pointed stars stand out distinctly or merge with the back-ground is dependent on the relationship of the colors. Where there is great contrast, the stars are easily visible; where there is little or no contrast, the star design recedes or some other pattern emerges. It is interesting to study each block for its individual artistic message.

To provide emphasis and contrast, strips of lush black velvet separate the blocks and surround the whole composition. And, to cap what must surely be considered a confection, an edging of handmade linen lace has been added.

6

SAMPLER

Salinda W. Rupp
Pieced cotton. 88×87¾".
c. 1870. Lancaster County, Pennsylvania.
Collection America Hurrah Antiques, New York City.

Salinda Rupp's encyclopedic sampler quilt is a prized and prime example of its type. Clearly inspired by, but not restricted to, traditional patchwork patterns, she assembled a collection of over 70 different blocks into a highly original and charming quilt that can easily be studied for hours.

There are many wonderful cotton fabrics in this piece, including the principal print used for the background—actually, sashing, or strips separating the squares—and the wide outer border. So masterful is Salinda Rupp's color sense that, although many hues and prints are represented, the overall effect is one of a carefully chosen scheme of just a few related colors, sparked by the occasional punch of bright yellow or red.

To assemble the quilt top, the quilter arranged the blocks and sashing diagonally. The red print squares that punctuate the sashing at regular intervals also serve to isolate and emphasize the individual blocks. At the edges, half-blocks and half-squares are used to fill in what would otherwise be triangular gaps. Notice that each half-block has its counterpart on the opposite side of the quilt—all, that is, except one—and the corners are filled in by quarter-blocks. Surrounding the large center area is a pieced zigzag border and a wide outside border.

It is fortunate that this beautiful quilt has survived to the present time: It is an eloquent testimonial to the imagination and skill of its creator.

7

STAIR STEPS OR ILLUSION

Ann Johnston
Pieced and embroidered silk, taffeta, and crepe. 70×81½".
c. 1890. Taylor County, Kentucky.
Collection The Kentucky Historical Society, Frankfort.

Thanks to a letter from Mrs. Elvira Johnston Wright, the niece of the quilter, we can attribute this quilt and gain some insight about its maker. The letter states:

> My aunt, Ann Johnston [1871–1964], made the quilt about 1890. She was born in Taylor County (Kentucky) and died in Oldham County. Her ancestors were pioneers in Green and Taylor counties. Her great-great-grandfather was Thomas Wheeler Edwards, who was a representative to the legislature from Green County in 1842. Aunt Ann's father was George Edwards Johnston [1835–1930], whose primary occupation was that of a farmer, although for several years he held an elective office in Taylor County as sheriff. Her mother was Mary Ellen Gaddie [1844–1917]. Ann was one of five sisters, the only one who married and left descendants. She was an expert seamstress, and for a while worked as a milliner in Louisville. Her handwork, including this quilt, won many prizes in county fairs.

This fascinating glimpse into the past helps us to understand and appreciate the artistry of Ann Johnston and her quilt. The design—consisting entirely of diamond-shaped bits of silky fabric, each one less than 1¼×2½"—is known as Stair Steps or, even more aptly, Illusion. It is actually the same as the *Pyramid Tumbling Blocks*, page 91; however, because of the color arrangement, the optical effect is more ambiguous. By shifting focus, it is possible to see tumbling blocks, stair steps, or six-pointed stars. The luminous, mosaic quality of the quilt is enhanced by feather-stitch embroidery covering the edges of every diamond-shaped patch.

8
WILLOW OAK

Appliquéd and pieced cotton. 92×72″.
c. 1840. Boston, Massachusetts.
The Shelburne Museum, Shelburne, Vermont;
gift of Electra Havemeyer Webb.

According to a previous owner, this quilt "was made in Boston on Beacon Street." It was found "wrapped in a handwoven sheet and a newspaper dated 1861 . . . packed away in a chest." Apparently in excellent condition despite (or because of) its storage, the quilt is a fine specimen of the appliqué technique. The color scheme, a dark blue calico print on white, not only makes the appliqué motifs stand out sharply but is also most pleasing to the eye.

Each of the 12 identical blocks is appliquéd with a medallion, which could be interpreted as either a snowflake or an abstract floral design, and four oak-leaf corner motifs. Pieced strips interspersed with tiny nine-patch checkerboards are used very effectively in setting the blocks together. All around the border, more oak leaves alternate with fanciful, treelike motifs. Some of these are obviously weeping willows; the others appear to be a variant of the medallion, somehow transformed into a tree. The arrangement, while not totally symmetrical, is carefully balanced.

In harmony with the rather severe discipline of the design, the quilting is as simple as possible. Each appliqué motif is outlined with stitching; the entire piece is then quilted in parallel diagonal rows. The quilting is worked exclusively on the white background. Perhaps the only touch of relaxation in this otherwise carefully controlled work is the small quilted heart in the center of each medallion.

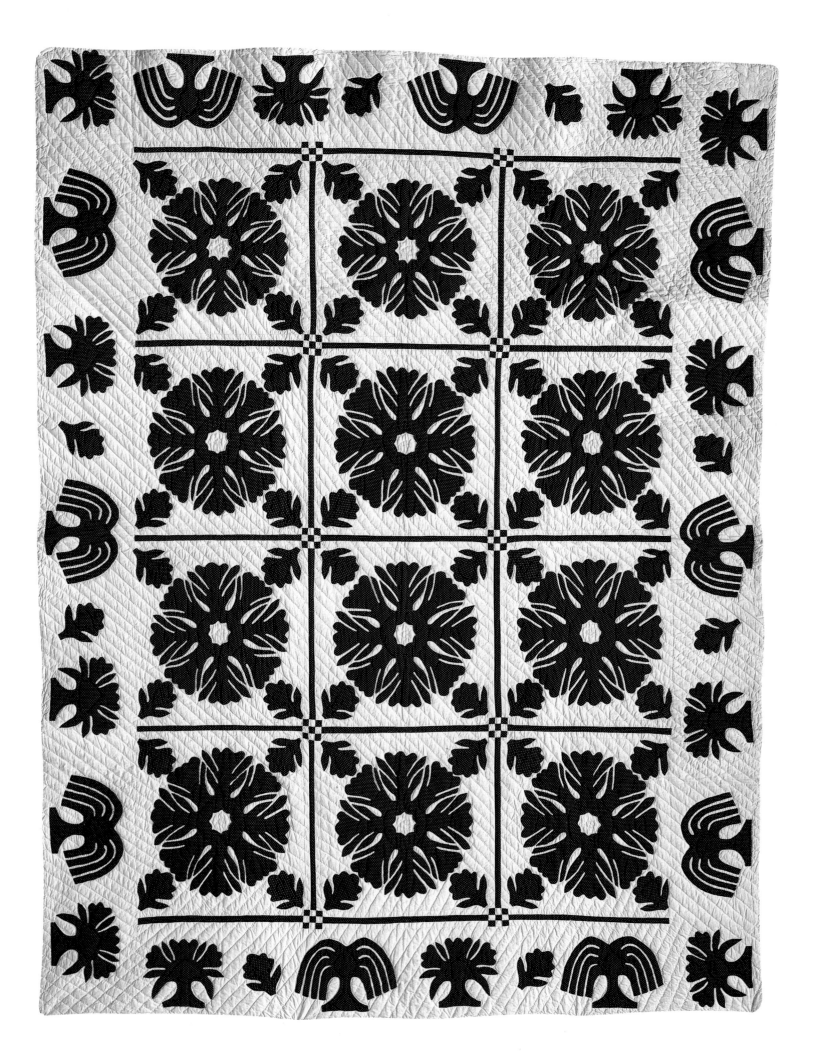

9

BASKET OF FLOWERS WITH FLORAL VINE
Appliquéd cotton sateen. 86×78".
c. 1930. Pennsylvania.
Private collection.
Courtesy Thos. K. Woodard American Antiques & Quilts, New York City.

Cotton sateen, with its soft sheen, adds its own note of luxury to this already refined and opulent quilt. This fabric was highly favored for making fancy quilts during the 1930s. The pale green background and the slightly muted yet rich colors of the appliqué also make this piece a textile of exceptional elegance.

The focal point of the quilt is a massive bouquet of tulips, arranged in a basket that has actually been woven from strips of fabric. The basket, a work of art in itself, is completely authentic, down to the rope-twist handle so characteristic of this style. The tulips, in their spring finery of red, yellow, pink, and mauve, are shaded and positioned so naturally that they invite comparison with their natural counterparts: Some are tightly closed, others are partially or completely open; some stand tall, others bend or droop, just as they might in real life. The coloring, the composition, and the fine stitchery are all masterful.

More long-stemmed tulips form the delicate vine that snakes its way around the perimeter of the quilt, making occasional contact with the elaborately scalloped border. The entire background is covered with finely stitched diamond quilting, with the exception of the wreath of tulips—a subtle paraphrase of the border vine. This is truly a shining example of the arts of appliqué and quilting.

10

BIBLE

Appliquéd and embroidered velvet and wool. 76×71″.
c. 1860–1890.
Place of origin unknown.
Collection America Hurrah Antiques, New York City.

Pale blue wool forms the backdrop for this lavishly detailed biblical pageant. The appliqués, including very convincing animal shapes, were cut from silk velvet, painstakingly arranged and applied to the background with tiny stitches. Touches of embroidery enrich the shapes and add lifelike textures.

Among the biblical themes illustrated, the one of Noah's Ark is most notable. Sitting solidly in the center and looking more like an English manor house than a boat, it draws pairs of animals from all sides like a magnet. In order to appreciate the remaining Bible stories and other decorations, the viewer should look at the quilt from different angles. At the upper left is the Garden of Eden with two angels; above the ark and upside down in relation to it is the Crucifixion. Additional biblical motifs, visible to those with a sharp eye, are Sodom and Gomorrah in flames, the Burning Bush, the Flight to Egypt, Jacob's Ladder, and the Golden Calf.

There are numerous clusters of buildings scattered about the quilt, no doubt representing settlements or cities. Embroidered details highlight the amusingly anachronistic architecture that, with its arcades and steeples, seems to belong more to Colonial America (note the Redcoats on horseback at the upper right) than to the lands of the Bible. Just inside the black velvet binding is a fine scalloped border, also in black, with a single animal nestled in each scallop.

11 CRAZY QUILT

Pieced and embroidered silk, satin, and velvet. 75×76".
c. 1880. Place of origin unknown.
The Museum of American Folk Art, New York City;
gift of Margaret Cavigga.

Crazy quilts are made either by joining pieces into a large whole or by assembling individual blocks and then joining these into a larger square or rectangle. In the present example, there are 49 separate blocks, each one unique. Most of these are assembled from the irregularly shaped pieces so typical of the crazy-quilt technique, but there are also a few plain—that is, unpieced—blocks. There is also one block, just above the center, featuring a beautiful multicolor Dresden Plate, a favorite traditional patchwork motif. Silk, satin, and velvet, all luxury fabrics, are used throughout, including the double border with its fine diamond quilting.

This quilt is exceptionally rich in embroidery. In addition to the feather stitching found on most crazy quilts, at least a dozen other embroidery stitches are employed, including cross-stitch, herringbone, satin, outline, lazy-daisy, French knot, and long-and-short, plus variations of these. The embroidery, in many colors, is used not only to embellish the seam lines of the piecing but also to create floral, animal, and other designs. Therefore, it is a major component, rather than a mere adjunct, of the work. Even though the embroidered child-figures, animals, and flowers were probably copied from commercial mail-order patterns, the quilt itself is unquestionably original in concept and execution. It is clear that the maker had a colorful imagination and was not in the least inhibited about using it.

12 CRAZY QUILT

Florence Elizabeth Marvin
Pieced, appliquéd, and embroidered silk and velvet. 80×76″.
1886. Brooklyn Heights, New York.
Collection America Hurrah Antiques, New York City.

Here is a veritable fantasy land in fabric, replete with birds and other animals, butterflies, and flowers. Florence Elizabeth Marvin's ornate crazy quilt is assembled from 16 irregular blocks, some roughly square, others rectangular. Almost every bit of silk or velvet making up the blocks has been lavishly embroidered or appliquéd or both. Even the black velvet border is alive with a serpentine vine of colorful flowers.

Many of the animals are padded, and the flowers, too, are appliquéd using a special three-dimensional technique. All are wonderfully detailed and lifelike. Adding to the realism is the use of velvet or other pile fabrics for the bodies of some of the animals to suggest the texture of fur or feathers. The quilt is thus a tactile as well as a visual treat, for surely no one could resist touching it. In one of the blocks (in the lower left quadrant), there is a stuffed hand gently grasping a fringed silk scarf—an acknowledgment, perhaps, that this is a quilt meant to be touched. A few inanimate objects—such as fans, an armchair, and a pitcher—are embroidered and tucked here and there among the flora and fauna.

In studying this quilt carefully, the viewer can see that Florence Marvin used a number of designs over and over again. A high-stepping waterfowl, a strutting rooster, and a wide-eyed owl are just a few of the repeated motifs. But each is a different color, with its own embellishments, so each one is unique—exactly as in nature.

13 KALEIDOSCOPE

Pieced and appliquéd cotton. 85×85″.
c. 1910. New Jersey.
Collection America Hurrah Antiques, New York City.

Uniquely conceived and masterfully executed, this striking quilt brings together two distinct artistic styles and two construction techniques. Working in red and white for maximum contrast, the quilter has created a piece that successfully combines Op Art with Art Nouveau, patchwork with appliqué.

Almost like a marble mosaic floor, the central kaleidoscope design appears to whirl dizzily from the center by means of ever larger "tiles"—in this case, fabric patches. These are skillfully cut into shapes that appear to be roughly square but are actually slightly flared, in order to fit their neighbors exactly and form larger and larger concentric circles. The patches of the outermost circle are very slightly rounded so that the perimeter of the circle will be a smooth, curved line. This is a perfect optical illusion.

The quilter's appliqué technique is no less impressive. There is in each corner an ornamental arabesque, strongly suggestive of a butterfly alighting for a brief rest, while the intermediate spaces are filled with pairs of simpler curlicues. Quilting is minimal: The geometric patches are x'd through with fine stitching, and the curved forms are outlined. The quilt is then finished off with a narrow red binding. It is a pity that the creator of this beautiful work of art remains anonymous.

14 Rainbow Monogram and Initial
Ida W. Beck
Appliquéd and embroidered cotton. 94×90".
1952–1954. Easton, Pennsylvania.
The Shelburne Museum, Shelburne, Vermont; gift of Ida W. Beck.

The creator of this marvelous quilt, Ida W. Beck, described herself as "over 70 years old, a shut-in since childhood," and went ón to say that she had always done needlework, with monogramming as her specialty. Referring to this quilt, she said, "It is quite original and I was several years in planning and making it." Astonishingly rich in detail, the quilt is a treasure trove of stitchery. It exemplifies not only painstaking appliqué and embroidery but also elaborate quilting to hold the layers together. It is worth examining the design for its many fascinating elements.

At the top of the center panel, there is a Gothic alphabet, followed by a motto and an arch formed by another alphabet. Directly below, in the center of the quilt, is a large design consisting of ornate, intertwined capital letters, underlined by a lower-case script alphabet. This is followed by Ida Beck's monogram/name, including the date and place of origin and yet another alphabet. Finally, there is one more alphabet worked in the form of a tree; over and around the tree are the days of the week, the seasons, and the directions of the wind. Two different alphabets, each embellished with spirals and flowers, run along either side of the center panel.

Along the sides, Ida Beck has embroidered the months of the year. Each month is accompanied by seasonal flowers, with a notation of that month's birthstone and important holidays. One side bears the legend "Good Morning," the other side "Good Night." Complementing and enlivening the design are numerous bluebirds flitting among the flowers.

We have already mentioned the superior quilting. What with the several patterns used—plumes, diamonds, flowers, and leaves, in both parallel and radiating rows—hardly an inch is left unquilted. Even the binding has been worked in the minutest detail; its curves and colors are a miniature echo of the appliquéd scallops that frame the principal design area.

16

SAMPLER
Pieced and appliquéd cotton. 92×88″.
c. 1850. Sheffield, Massachusetts.
Collection America Hurrah Antiques, New York City.

Exuberant, fresh, and *colorful* are all terms that can be used to characterize the sampler quilt pictured here. Still in fine condition despite its age, it is a reference work of many different patchwork patterns. Largest and most prominent are the six Compass blocks, assembled from circular, triangular, and kite-shaped pieces in various prints. Diamonds, triangles, and squares figure importantly in the numerous smaller blocks and bands that surround and accompany the Compass blocks. Among the patterns represented are Flying Geese, Broken Dishes, Pinwheel, Arrowhead, Four-Patch, Window Pane, and Pieced Star. A narrow zigzag band bisects the central area vertically, and on either side of the same area, there is a panel in the Grandmother's Flower Garden pattern, made up entirely of small hexagons.

Interestingly, the quilt is bordered on only three sides—first by a narrow red band, then by a wide appliquéd border. This outer border has an undulating, leafy green vine, with flowers in red and yellow, all on a white background. It offers a sharp contrast in both color and feeling to the inner patchwork area. The entire piece is quilted: In the sampler area, the stitching follows the various patchwork shapes. The red inner border is diamond quilted, and the outer border is quilted in parallel diagonal rows, with a chevron at the bottom center to aid in shifting direction. A unique tricolor piping in red, green, and yellow is inserted between the quilt and the binding to finish the edges.

17 Pieced and Appliquéd Quilt

Martha Hewitt
Pieced and appliquéd cotton. 80×72".
1855. Michigan.
Collection America Hurrah Antiques, New York City.

Martha Hewitt had every right to be proud of her work, as her embroidered signature, along with "Age 56 Michigan 1855," attests. The design is original, colorful, and delightfully folksy. An immense medallion in the center, dominated by a compass motif, is the focal point. Assembled by a technique that combines piecing and appliqué, the compass is encircled by a blue field perforated with stars (or suns) and crescent moons. In a further reference to the heavens, a series of rainbows forms a scalloped edging around the blue field. To finish the medallion, thin red spokes have been inserted between the rainbows, radiating outward to a red-and-white sawtoothed rim.

The flag-bearing soldiers at the quilt's corners are another intriguing motif. They are stylized but convincingly detailed, their coats minutely embroidered to denote gold braid, pocket flaps, buttons, and epaulettes. The flags are pieced (note the chevroned stripes, which suggest a breeze) and are embroidered with stars. Other appliqué motifs include flowers, crossed mallets, and dividers superimposed on T squares.

Along three sides of the border, Martha Hewitt has appliquéd pots bursting with fantasy flowers; she has indicated texture and shading by the skillful use of solid and print fabrics. The top border incorporates the quilter's signature, and the bottom and sides are edged with bicolored scalloping. Altogether, this is a most joyful and enjoyable representative of the quilting art.

18

BABY'S PLAYTHINGS
Pieced, appliquéd, and embroidered wool and silk. 33×46″.
c. 1880. Midwest.
Courtesy Thos. K. Woodard American Antiques & Quilts, New York City.

This well-worn and undoubtedly much-loved baby quilt is a
charming example of the use of several different needlework
techniques to create a unified whole. Worked in wool and
silk fabrics, the quilt has a crazy-quilt center, a simple pieced
border, and a wealth of appliquéd and embroidered pictorial
motifs and lettering.

The appliquéd motifs are of special interest. While the name
of the quilt suggests that the pictured objects were playthings
for a child, obviously not all of them could have been. It is
more likely that they were part of the child's larger world,
familiarly observed. The presence of domestic and barnyard
animals implies that the family lived on a farm; other every-
day objects—such as a watering can, coffee grinder, watch,
and ladder—reinforce the image of an ordinary farm household. Many of the appliquéd designs, while easily identifiable
merely from their shapes, are cut without regard to true color
or scale: a blue dog and a red rabbit, a horse and a fish of the
same size. These aberrations, of course, in no way detract
from the appeal of the design. The quilt is omnidirectional;
that is, because the appliquéd designs face in different directions, it should be viewed from all sides.

Embroidery is used here to good effect. Both the crazy-quilt
patches and the borders are embellished with double feather
stitching, as is the large center patch with *Baby* spelled out in
bold letters for all who might be in doubt. Both the appliquéd
motifs and the lettering are held in place with contrasting
blanket stitches, a technique that eliminates the need to turn
under the raw edges. Finer details are worked in outline
stitches and French knots. We can only speculate about the
initials *I.K.W.*; the most likely conclusion is that they are
those of the quilt's maker.

19 CRIB QUILT TOP

Pieced and appliquéd cotton. 38×38".
c. 1885. New York.
Collection America Hurrah Antiques, New York City.

Quilt or picture? Not much over a yard square, it was probably intended as the top of a crib quilt, but it could just as well have been framed and displayed on a wall. Many colorful calico prints, as well as solids, stripes, and plaids, went into this delightful work, which abounds in whimsical touches.

An appliquéd farmhouse of striped ticking is complete with windows, a sloping roof, and two smoking chimneys. In the doorway stands a figure, no doubt a mother watching over her children at play in the nearby field. The figures of the mother, children, and dog appear to have been cut out of a print and appliquéd to the background. At the lower right of the field, perhaps being chased by the dog, are two liveried rabbits with a wheelbarrow full of Easter eggs. The print chosen to represent the field, incidentally, is a clever one: The wavy stripes suggest furrows (albeit crooked ones!). And instead of trees, two flowered columns, each topped by a gigantic but friendly bird, flank the house. There is even a board fence consisting of vertical strips in various prints and solids and, of course, a gate—here, closed for security. Although the sky is light, suggesting daytime, stars are visible —and why not? In the land of make-believe, there is no need to be too literal.

The cozy, homey scene is enclosed in a patchwork border made up of alternating blocks in a miniature plaid and a four-patch variation. Its total effect is one of simple, cheerful, unsophisticated charm.

20 Alphabets

Yvonne M. Khin
Pieced, appliquéd, and embroidered cotton. 58×52".
1984. Bethesda, Maryland.
Collection the artist.

Utilizing her considerable skills in piecing, appliqué, and embroidery, Yvonne M. Khin designed and executed *Alphabets* in honor of her grandnephew Stephen Axe. She felt that it would be an attractive and effective teaching tool to help him learn both the alphabet and the numbers from one to ten. Indeed, any child would find this quilt irresistible.

Five horizontal off-white panels—four for the alphabet and one for the numbers—constitute the background for the design. Each pale blue letter contains appliquéd and embroidered objects whose names begin with that letter. The letter *R*, for example, displays a rhinoceros, radishes, a rabbit, a raccoon, a rose, a rat, a pair of reindeer, a ring, and a robin. Each item is so convincingly detailed that it is instantly recognizable. The numbers panel illustrates each numeral with the appropriate quantity of objects, from one elephant to ten trees. By means of these lessons, the child can learn not only to recognize the various letters and numbers, but also to understand what they represent.

To complete the design, Yvonne Khin has used dark blue-green bands to separate the panels and to form the border. The quilting, too, enhances the work. On the alphabet panels, parallel rows of stitching outline the various letters, and on the bottom panel, quilted stars are scattered among the appliquéd motifs. The bands are quilted in white thread with a birds-and-hearts pattern, the border with sprigs of flowers. This exuberant, lively quilt is surely a labor of love.

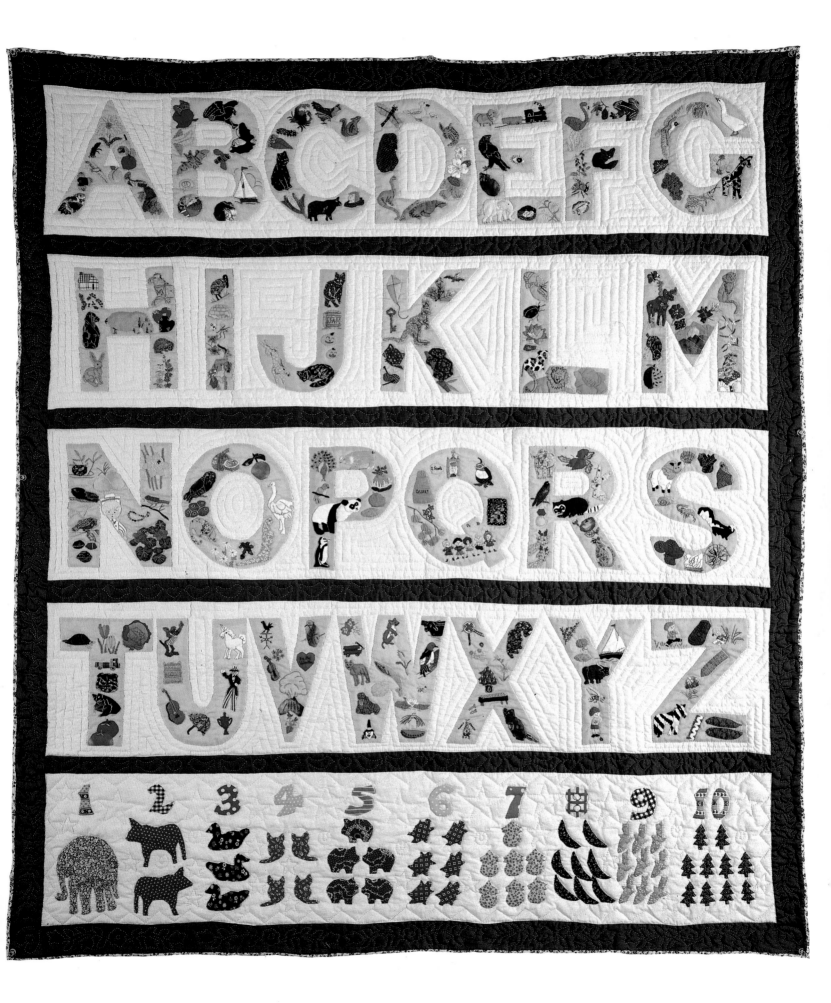

21 BLACK-FAMILY ALBUM

Sarah Ann Wilson
Appliquéd, embroidered, and pieced cotton. 85×100″.
1854. New York or New Jersey.
Private collection; courtesy America Hurrah Antiques,
New York City.

Using delightfully primitive, stylized motifs and clear colors, Sarah Ann Wilson created this rare and beautiful pictorial quilt. Each of the 30 appliquéd blocks depicts a different scene. There are animals, people (probably members of her family), houses (perhaps including her own), and many fanciful bouquets of flowers. The human figures, being black, are especially effective because they stand out like silhouettes against the creamy background. A closer look will reveal touches of embroidery on these figures, suggesting facial features and clothing details. Subtle embroidery appears in several other blocks, too, denoting, for example, veins of leaves or crosshatching on a vase of flowers.

In assembling her quilt, Sarah Ann Wilson separated the picture blocks with narrow strips, or sashing, of a contrasting print, piecing them all together in the manner of a multi-paned window. The quilting itself, done in thread to match the background, is as individual as each block, echoing the outline or contours of each particular motif, while at the same time completely filling in the background of the block.

While most quilts are finished with a simple binding around the edges, this one departs from tradition by having a double scalloped edging, meticulously bound with narrow bias strips cut from the same fabric as the sashing. A little appliquéd bull's-eye highlighting each scallop is the final, whimsical touch.

22 BALTIMORE ALBUM

Hannah Foote
Appliquéd and pieced cotton. 104×104″.
1850. Baltimore, Maryland.
Collection America Hurrah Antiques, New York City.

Since Hannah Foote signed and dated her quilt, a practice unfortunately too often omitted, we know exactly whom to pay tribute to when admiring the work. This is a very large piece—almost three yards on a side—and it surely represents many hours of stitchery. The design comprises 25 blocks, each one different, joined to narrow, red-print strips (sashing) that both separate and frame the blocks.

The blocks can be divided roughly into three types: pictorial, naturalistic floral, and stylized floral, although in a few cases these categories overlap. Those with human or animal figures can be classified as pictorial, especially the central block, which depicts a cow being milked, along with a dog and two ducks. Two blocks over to the right, another bucolic scene portrays a girl out for a walk, a basket on her arm and her dog scampering behind her. Examples of the naturalistic floral blocks include those picturing a bouquet of flowers in a vase or basket, or a wreath or bunch of flowers without a container. The stylized florals are those whose shapes and colors have been reduced to a few suggestive elements, arranged in a formal or symmetrical composition. Despite the disparity in their approach to design, the various blocks seem to work as a whole, held together by the white background, the use of a few bright, clear colors, and the execution, particularly the bits of embroidery defining some of the small details.

An intricate, stepped-sawtooth border, which repeats the red print of the sashing, surrounds the blocks. The entire white portion of the quilt is covered with close, almost minute, diamond quilting. In every respect, Hannah Foote has produced a prime specimen of the Baltimore Album quilt.

23 MARYLAND ALBUM

Appliquéd cotton. 98×101″.
c. 1840. Maryland.
The Shelburne Museum, Shelburne, Vermont;
gift of Electra Havemeyer Webb.

Pictured here is another lovely album quilt from Maryland, generally conceded to have produced the finest examples of this type. This well-preserved quilt is from about 1840, a few years before the full flowering of the album quilt genre. Colorful and beautifully stitched, the quilt was awarded first prize at the Maryland State Fair of 1939.

Each of the 25 motifs is appliquéd on a separate block. Except for the four corner blocks, which depict pineapples (the symbol of hospitality), the motifs are all different. They are mostly floral or botanical, the exceptions being the center motif of a prancing horse—an image both familiar and appropriate to the state of Maryland—and the many flying birds. The overflowing cornucopia, the fat sheaf of wheat, and the tree loaded with fruit all attest to what must have been a prosperous period.

After the blocks were set together, additional birds were appliquéd here and there, contributing further to the joyfulness and freedom of the composition. Two red borders separated by a white border frame the design, and a narrow white binding finishes the edges. The fine appliqué is enhanced by close outline quilting, varying from block to block according to the motif. The borders are quilted in a pyramidal pattern.

24 ALBUM

Appliquéd, embroidered, and pieced cotton. 96×93".
c. 1850. New York.
Private collection; courtesy Thos. K. Woodard American
Antiques & Quilts, New York City.

Although album quilts are primarily associated with the state of Maryland and even more specifically with the city of Baltimore, such quilts were made elsewhere as well. The one shown here came from New York State, and it is a very good representative of that type, which flourished around the middle of the nineteenth century.

This particular quilt consists of 143 blocks, each one illustrating a different botanical or zoological subject. Among the numerous flowers, leaves, fruits, birds, and animals, there are to be found even a starfish and a wormlike creature. Although the appliquéd designs are somewhat stylized and simplified, the quilter has chosen her colors and prints carefully to suggest the actual tones and textures of nature. A number of blocks carry a helpful embroidered caption identifying the specimen: snipe, eagle, moose, hog, elephant, and so on. One only wishes that all the blocks had been similarly labeled, especially some of the flowers.

Each block is framed by a dark calico print used uniformly throughout; the blocks are then set together with red sashing. Both the sashing and the blocks are quilted—the latter individually, according to the shape of the motif. An unobtrusive, though unifying, double border, consisting of the same dark print and solid red, finishes off the quilt nicely.

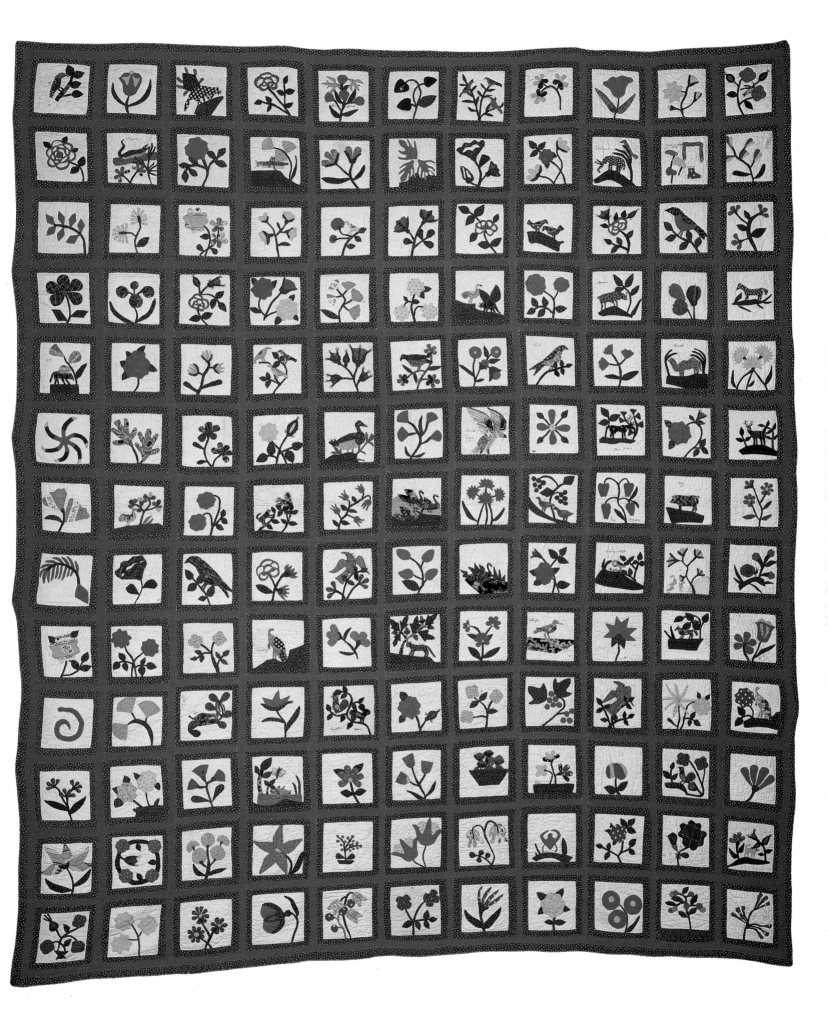

25 KALEIDOSCOPE COLOR

Appliquéd, pieced, and embroidered cotton and synthetics. 80×65″.
1982. Nationwide.
Fairfield Processing Quilt Collection, Fairfield, Connecticut.

This quilt came about as a result of the 1982 quilt block contest sponsored by the Fairfield Processing Corporation, a manufacturer of quilt batting and related products. Prize-winning blocks were collected from all over the country and were joined into the quilt pictured here; the grand-prize-winning block, by Sheryl Hinsdale, is in the third row from the top, second block from the left.

With the exception of three pictorial squares, the blocks strongly evoke the kaleidoscopic qualities suggested by the quilt's title. Using only solid colors (a contest requirement), each designer arranged her bits of fabric into sparkling, mosaiclike bursts of color that seem to be illuminated by some inner light. Just as a kaleidoscope yields an infinite variety of patterns, the variety of these motifs reminds us that the possibilities of quilt block design are infinite.

Both patchwork and appliqué techniques are represented here. Some of the designs appear to have been inspired by traditional patterns, but they have been so freshly interpreted and reworked that they give the impression of total original-ity. Several of the blocks are further enhanced by hand em-broidery; the merry-go-round horse is particularly rich in embroidered touches. Each block carries its own quilting, usually following the contours of the design.

26 Centennial

G. Knappenberger
Pieced and appliquéd cotton. 71½×83½".
1876. Pennsylvania.
The Museum of American Folk Art, New York City;
gift of Rhea Goodman.

It is doubtful that many quilts were made to celebrate our country's Bicentennial. A hundred years before, however, a commemorative quilt was a common symbol of recognition for our *first* century. In the example shown here, the Centennial shares equal billing with the quilter, G. Knappenberger, whose name appears in bold letters not once but twice.

The colors in this quilt are limited: There are only five, and they are somewhat muted. But they contrast nicely with the white background and, along with the exuberant design, they produce an effect that is anything but subdued. The large center motif features a pieced feathered star, embellished with stylized flowers and the all-important date. Other motifs include additional stylized flowers, hearts, stars, and patchwork baskets with birds. At either side of the large central area is a bold zigzag border in pink and green. Along the outer edges, the top and bottom borders are similar, with birds perched on leafy branches and the lettering mentioned before. The side borders are not the same, however. On the left, a row of fanciful flowers seems to grow out of the adjacent zigzag border, whereas on the right, two flowering stalks issue from the corners and meet in the middle. The apparently intentional disregard of strict symmetry as well as the other delightful eccentricities of this quilt endow it with humor and joyfulness—appropriate emotions for the occasion it commemorates.

27

CENTRAL MEDALLION *CONSTITUTION*
Appliquéd, embroidered, and pieced cotton. 73×66".
c. 1860–1880. Place of origin unknown.
Collection America Hurrah Antiques, New York City.

While the large center motif picturing the frigate *Constitution* is undeniably the focal point, there are many other fascinating subjects depicted in this album quilt.

First of all, there are many animal, bird, and floral motifs, both realistic and abstract, as well as a few popular quilt motifs—for example, the heart-in-hand design above the upper-right-hand corner of the center motif. Then there are biblical themes: Adam and Eve, Cain and Abel, King David with His Harp, Abraham Sacrificing Isaac, and Noah's Ark. Finally, there are historical/political blocks, for example, portraits believed to be of presidents James A. Garfield (centered above the *Constitution*), Ulysses S. Grant (bottom row), and Abraham Lincoln (next to the groom in the large wedding block). To the right of the center motif is a block showing a man seated at a desk; because of the resemblance to pictures of the *Constitution*'s captain, it is thought to be his portrait. In addition to all these, other human figures and inanimate objects abound, although their significance, if any, is unknown. Not to be missed is the border of birds, a veritable encyclopedia on the subject.

It is interesting to note that the individual blocks, which are painstakingly appliquéd and embroidered (some of the men's clothes are incredibly detailed, even to their turned-back lapels), are quite irregular in size and shape. Many of the blocks have been pieced around the edges with narrow strips in order to make them the same size as their neighbors. These imperfections, of course, only heighten the charm and personal appeal of this extraordinary quilt.

28 Graveyard

Elizabeth Roseberry Mitchell
Pieced, appliquéd, and embroidered cotton. 85×81″.
1839. Lewis County, Kentucky.
Collection The Kentucky Historical Society, Frankfort.

The very idea of commemorating death by means of a decorative textile is surely an alien one to us in the 1980s. A century and a half ago, however, this macabre practice was common enough. Embroidered mourning pictures, depicting a bereaved widow—often surrounded by her children—grieving at her husband's tombstone beneath a dripping weeping willow, were found in many a Victorian parlor. In this context, Elizabeth Roseberry Mitchell's Graveyard quilt is not at all out of place. Mrs. Mitchell, who had lived in Ohio and buried two young sons there, later moved to Kentucky, where she was inspired to create her quilt.

The background is an uncomplicated pattern of print patches alternating with LeMoyne Star blocks. The subdued browns and beiges are appropriate to the somber theme, which is graphically illustrated by the fenced-in graveyard at the center and by the numerous appliquéd coffins along the border. Each coffin carries a paper tag with the name of a family member. The intent was to move the coffin into the graveyard when that person died. (Four coffins, including those for the two children, have already made the journey.) Along the top, bottom, and right side of the border, even the quilting is coffin shaped, sometimes with a double outline. Along the left side, the quilting has been modified to a mere suggestion of the coffin shape.

In addition to the picket fence around the graveyard, with its elaborate, arched gateway, there are similar fences along the path leading to the cemetery and around the outer edge of the quilt, outside the coffin border. In an effort to lighten the dreary mood, or perhaps to acknowledge that life must go on, Mrs. Mitchell embroidered vines with pink flowers along certain stretches of the fence.

29

MASONIC RIBBON
Pieced and embroidered silk and velvet. 66½×56½".
c. 1890. Kentucky.
Collection The Kentucky Historical Society, Frankfort.

What a creative way to display a collection of Masonic ribbons! These are souvenirs from the order of Knights Templar, and they come from lodges located in many towns and cities in several states, among them Ohio, Pennsylvania, Texas, Michigan, Kansas, Tennessee, Maryland, and, of course, Kentucky. Most of the ribbons that bear dates are from the 1870s. Several are printed with the names of committees or activities, such as Finance, Reception, and Location of Tables.

The design of the quilt top radiates from a large central block, a square of velvet embroidered with the cross-and-crown emblem of the Knights Templar and edged with fancy embroidery. Lengths of silk and velvet ribbon are joined to the sides of this block to form a short-armed cross. To fill in the rest of the quilt, the ribbons are laid edge to edge, overlapping slightly. Yellow-gold, red, purple, and other colors of embroidery thread—probably pearl cotton—are used to join the edges by means of feather stitching. The tiers of joined ribbons are separated by narrow red ribbon, also edged with embroidery. Eight solid squares of velvet, echoing the central block, are incorporated into the design in a stepped arrangement that leads the eye to the corners of the quilt. The border is made of the same reddish-brown velvet and is also feather stitched along both edges. In terms of conception and execution, this is certainly a fine example of the commemorative quilt.

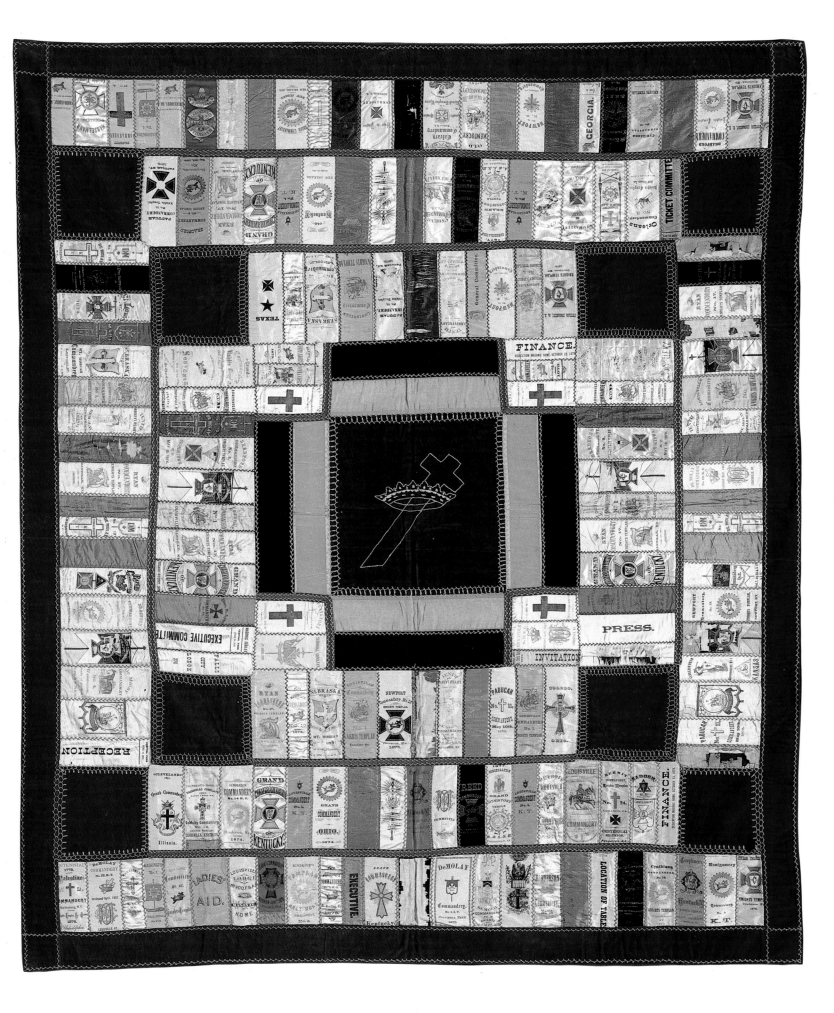

30

TIPPECANOE

Pieced cotton. 79×79″. c. 1890s. Place of origin unknown.
The Shelburne Museum, Shelburne, Vermont;
gift of Miss Anna Colman, Boston.

Political campaigns of the late nineteenth century often inspired the printing of topical fabrics, handkerchiefs, and other textiles. These, in turn, were frequently made into quilts, such as the one shown here. This one commemorates the successful campaign for the presidency and vice-presidency, respectively, of Benjamin Harrison and Levi P. Morton, who served from 1889 to 1893. The name *Tippecanoe* is a throwback to the 1840 presidential campaign of Harrison's grandfather, William Henry Harrison, who was nicknamed Old Tippecanoe in honor of his exploits in the Battle of Tippecanoe (1811) against the Indians. His memorable campaign slogan, "Tippecanoe and Tyler Too," included the name of John Tyler, his running mate, who assumed the presidency when Harrison died just a month after taking the oath of office.

This quilt in honor of Benjamin Harrison (who served his full term) is extremely simple in design. It is pieced together, diamond-fashion, from handkerchiefs—or bandannas, as each is about 20 inches square—of two different patterns. There are nine complete squares and nine more that have been cut into halves or quarters. The squares could easily have been joined by machine, since only straight stitching is involved. However, the square, or box, quilting was done by hand, with very regular, small stitches. As a nice finishing touch, the quilter bound the edges in a shade of blue that almost exactly matches the background of the portrait squares.

31 GLORIOUS LADY FREEDOM

Moneca Calvert
Pieced, appliquéd, and embroidered cotton. 72×72".
1986. Carmichael, California.
The Museum of American Folk Art, New York City.

A masterpiece of conception, composition, and color, Moneca Calvert's highly personal, yet universal, tribute to the Statue of Liberty on the occasion of its centennial won the $20,000 first prize in Scotchgard's Great American Quilt Contest. In the designer's own words:

> I first visited the Statue of Liberty in 1982 and wanted a design with the same visual impact as the real thing: For that reason, I wanted the figure of the statue to dominate and be as close to human size as possible. . . . I chose to do a bird's-eye view with the landscape of the purple mountains and the fields of grain receding into the horizon.

How well she has succeeded in transforming her vision into a vivid and graphic textile reality!

The Stars and Stripes, snapping in the breeze, seems to grow directly out of the landscape of gently rolling hills, towering mountains, and fertile fields fading into the distance. Especially notable are the effective use of random-dyed fabrics to denote the colors and textures of mountains and sky, the naturalistic piecing, and the varied patterns of hand quilting.

In the foreground, Lady Liberty rises up as though unwrapped from the flag, proudly holding her torch aloft. Subtle shapings and shadings of green and black not only suggest the folds of her drapery but also emphasize the sculptural quality of the figure. The small vignette of New York harbor in the lower-right corner depicts the distinctive skyline of lower Manhattan, establishing the Lady in her familiar home. Significant, too, is the hand-embroidered legend "from sea to shining sea"—the soul-stirring phrase from *America the Beautiful.*

32 Lei Mamo (Mamo Lei)

Appliquéd cotton. 80×80″.
Late nineteenth century. Hawaiian Islands.
Honolulu Academy of Arts; gift of Damon Giffard.

No one knows for sure how or when Hawaiian quilts originated. Native islanders made a type of cloth from the inner bark of plants that they used for such textiles as clothing and bed coverings. The latter usually consisted of several layers, and the top layer was decorated with brightly painted designs. After the arrival of merchants, traders, and missionaries in the late eighteenth century, commercially produced fabric became available. Missionary wives introduced the technique of quilting, which the islanders soon imitated and then adapted to their own style and purposes.

The quilt pictured here was once owned by the grandmother of the donor, a descendant of the Brickwood family, for whom it was made. It was a prizewinner in a 1943 competition held in conjunction with the "Hawaii Farm as Home" exhibition at the Honolulu Academy of Arts. It is a quite typical example of the native art, with its square shape, its characteristic center motif and border designs inspired by local vegetation, and its red-on-white color scheme. While Hawaiian quilts were made in all colors, red was one of the most commonly used, since turkey-red fabric (named for the country) was among the earliest and most popular commercial cloths available. The usual method of creating the appliqué design was to fold a large square of fabric into eighths, with the last fold forming a triangle. The border was cut first; then the center motif was cut from the remaining fabric. Sometimes paper patterns were used, but often the designs were cut freehand. The cutouts were then unfolded, pinned to the background, and appliquéd in place.

33

KU'U HAE ALOHA (MY BELOVED FLAG)
Pieced and appliquéd cotton. 85½×83″.
Before 1918. Waimea (Big Island).
Honolulu Academy of Arts; gift of Mrs. Richard Cooke.

To most people familiar with Hawaiian quilts, the image of
a large square with a contrasting symmetrical border and
center motif of stylized flowers and leaves, all appliquéd, is
what comes to mind. This quilt, however, is in another style
entirely. It represents a theme that was once highly popular
with native Hawaiians. In addition to expressing affection for
the national flag, this type of quilt is of special historical
interest, since it may predate United States possession of the
islands. During the 1840s, the Sandwich Islands, as they
were then known, were actually in British hands for a few
months. Although the British rule was short, the Union Jack
found its way onto the flag of Hawaii. Often, especially in
times of political stress, that flag would reemerge as a symbol
of national pride.

It is four such flags, pieced from red, white, and blue fabrics,
that form this quilt. The fifth major piece is a center block,
appliquéd with the Hawaiian coat of arms and an elaborately
draped bunting topped with a crown—a reminder that native kings and queens once reigned over the Islands. A few
touches of yellow and tan are added to enrich and contrast
with the basic red, white, and blue color scheme. And, in
case there should be any doubt, the Hawaiian words for "My
Beloved Flag" spell out the quilt's patriotic message. In keep-
ing with the mostly geometric shapes, all of the quilting is
based on straight lines. The center block is diamond quilted
throughout, and the stripes of the flags are diagonally quilted
in a chevron pattern. A plain white binding finishes the
edges neatly and unobtrusively.

34 Na Kalauno (Crowns)

Appliquéd cotton. 82½×81½".
Before 1918. Hawaiian Islands.
Honolulu Academy of Arts; gift of Mrs. C. M. Cooke Estate.

This lush quilt, based on the complementary colors yellow and purple, is in brilliant orange-yellow and strong lavender. As a result, the contrast is especially striking and possesses great depth and richness.

Instead of one large center motif and a related border, the appliqué design is made up of several smaller elements. The reduced center medallion, a highly stylized interpretation of indigenous blossoms and leaves, is wreathed by eight palm fronds with deeply notched edges. Taking the place of a border are eight regal crowns, one at each corner and the others centered between. These crowns, of course, commemorate the native monarchs of Hawaii's vanished kingdom. To obtain the appliqués, the quilter folded a square of fabric into eighths and, cutting each element once, produced the center motif and the eight palm fronds, but only four crowns. She would have had to cut the other four from leftovers. This probably accounts for the subtle differences between the corner crowns and the others.

Consistent with tradition, the quilting follows the shapes of the appliqués, in ever-receding, parallel rows of stitching. For this reason, it is sometimes called echo quilting. Those with a romantic turn of mind will find the local wisdom appealing: This quilting pattern actually represents the waves of the Pacific lazily lapping against the shores of the Islands.

35 Diamond In A Square

Pieced wool. 81×80″.

c. 1920. Lancaster County, Pennsylvania.

Collection America Hurrah Antiques, New York City.

This lovely quilt is a splendid example of Amish art and design. It is characteristic of its kind in a number of ways: fabric, colors, pattern, and quilting. Most Amish quilts from Pennsylvania are made from lightweight wool, either homespun or purchased. This one, dating from about 1920, is probably made from bought rather than homemade fabric. The subdued yet rich colors so characteristic of these quilts are skillfully combined here. Although Amish women were prohibited from dressing in bright colors, they were not so restricted when it came to their quilts. Hence, the bright red of the border and the touches of light blue are a welcome contrast to the somber dark green and mulberry shades that predominate.

Diamond in a Square is one of the most often used Amish patterns. It is merely a square turned on one of its corners to form a diamond and then placed within a larger square. In this version, both the diamond and the square have borders with contrasting small squares set into the corners. Finishing off the whole is the wide red outer border with large green blocks at the corners and a mulberry binding.

As in so many Amish quilts, intricate quilting stitches are used here to set off this otherwise rather simple piece. Because of its puffiness, the quilting shows up exceptionally well. In the center diamond, concentric six-pointed stars are surrounded by concentric wreaths. The square is filled in with closely spaced diamonds, and both narrow borders are quilted with little flowers. The quilting around the outer border is done in a feathered scroll pattern. In every way, this is an elegant quilt, particularly from the standpoint of simplicity and fine execution.

36

PUSS IN THE CORNER
Pieced wool and crepe. 79×80″.
c. 1920. Pennsylvania.
The Esprit Collection, San Francisco.

Executed in fine wools, this well-made Amish quilt from Pennsylvania utilizes a rather restricted color palette in an inventive manner. Different shades of blue, green, and purple are the principal colors, aided by a startling stab of brilliant coral at the center of each small motif. Another surprise is the single brown strip forming the lower edge of the inner border. One wonders whether the quilter ran out of green or was just being playful. In any case, it is a humorous note, not at all amiss in this well-balanced design.

The basis for the Puss in the Corner motif is the nine-patch pattern: nine small squares joined three-by-three to form another square. This is then joined to four rectangles and four squares (presumably the puss in the corner). There are three color variations of the motif in this quilt, each one achieved by changing only the color of the rectangular elements. The optical effect of each of the variations is quite different.

There are three quilting patterns in this piece. The motifs are diamond quilted, while the border and sashing (the strips separating the motifs) are worked in a simple chain. Around the outer border, closely spaced stitching forms connecting oval wreaths of wild roses and leaves. And, as is common in Amish quilts, the binding around the edge is of a contrasting color, in this case, black.

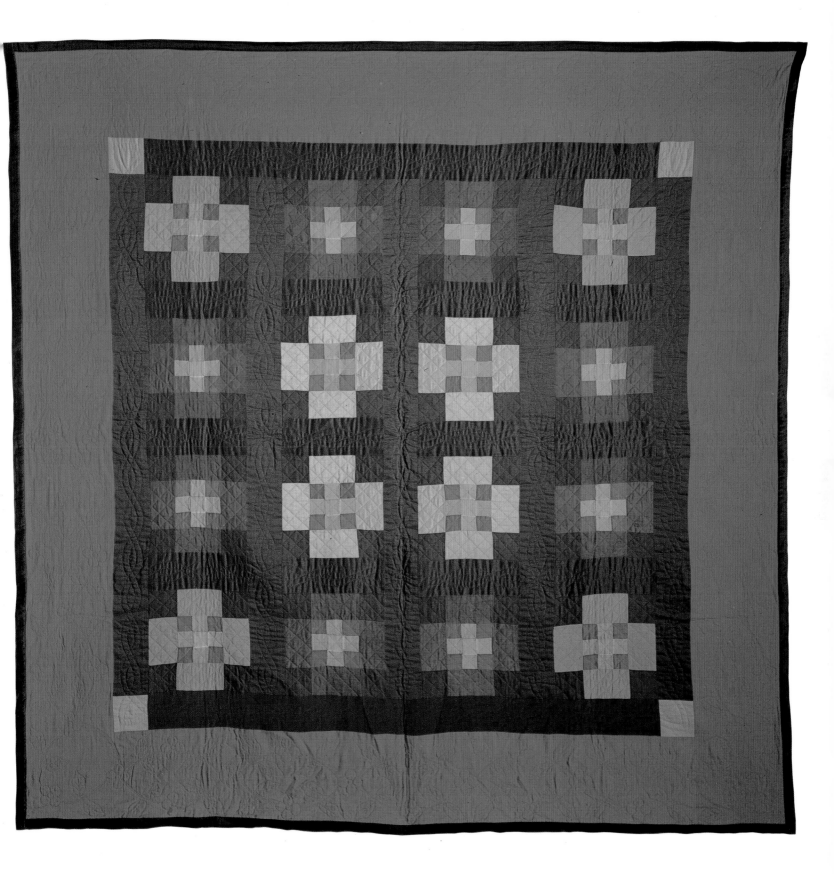

37

NINE-PATCH DIAMOND IN THE SQUARE
Pieced wool. 60×62".
c. 1900. Lancaster County, Pennsylvania.
Collection Bettie Mintz, Bethesda, Maryland.

Variations on the Diamond in the Square theme are seemingly endless. The diamond may be bordered, the square borderless—or vice versa. Both may have borders; both may lack them. The borders may have contrasting corners or not. The proportions and the colors of diamonds, squares, and borders may vary greatly. Each quilt maker can thus create a unique interpretation of this popular, basic pattern.

The Diamond in the Square quilt pictured here is quite rare. What makes it so unusual is that the diamond, rather than being a simple solid square turned 45 degrees, is instead made up of 13 nine-patch blocks and 12 solid blocks. And because some of the small corner elements of the nine-patch blocks are so similar in color to the larger solid blocks, they seem to recede into the background while pushing forward the light-gray X shapes.

Another exceptional feature of this quilt is the substantial outer border in bright red. Although other Amish quilts often have outer borders in bright or contrasting colors, they are seldom as startling as this one. The edges of the quilt are finished in the usual manner, with a narrow, contrasting binding. Incidentally, the quilter seems to have found it necessary to piece the brown square into which the diamond is set. Thanks to the translucent quality of the fabric, we can see just how she accomplished that feat.

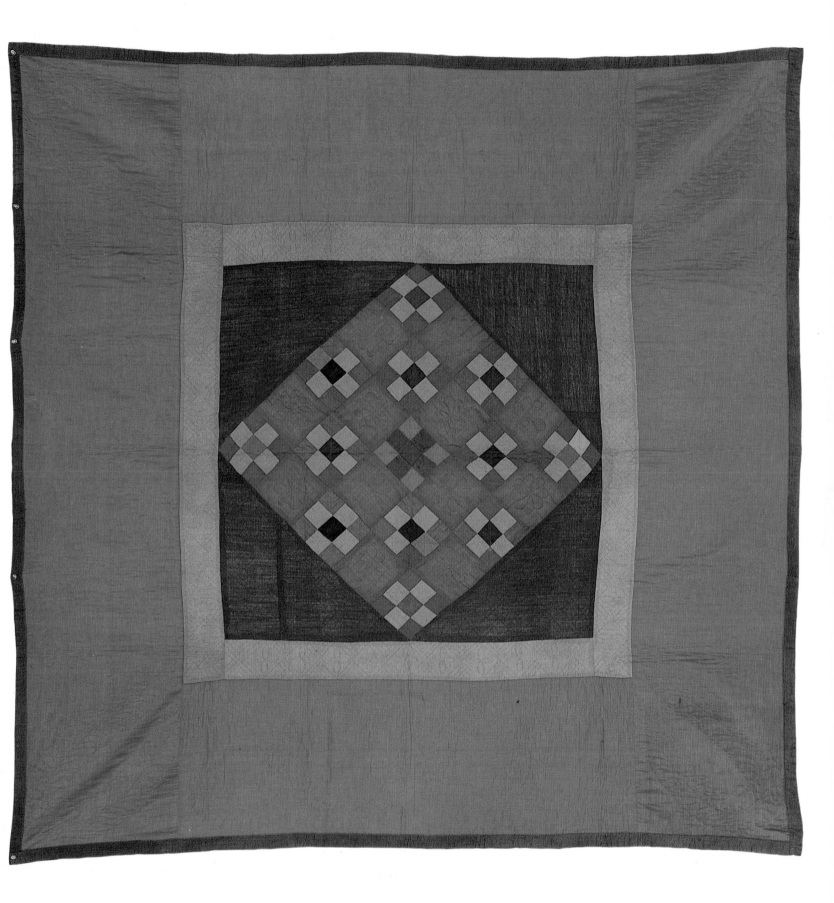

38 Pyramid Tumbling Blocks

Pieced cotton. 108×94".
c. 1935. Ohio.
Collection America Hurrah Antiques, New York City.

It is easy to see how this quilt came by its name. The Tumbling Blocks component refers to the pattern of optically three-dimensional cubes; the Pyramid to the deliberate color sequences and the arrangement of light and dark patches that creates the illusion of peaking pyramids. Compare this disciplined, purposeful version of the pattern with the Stair Steps, or Illusion, quilt on page 29, where the color placement is deliberately hit-or-miss. The total effect is entirely valid and pleasing in its own way.

Here, too, we see the use of a traditional patchwork pattern made up in cotton, a common practice among the Midwestern Amish. The Tumbling Blocks motif consists entirely of diamonds—not diagonal squares but true diamonds, with acute and obtuse angles. Great care is required in assembling them, in order to match the edges exactly and to ensure sharp corners. The person who made this quilt did a superb job in that respect, not to mention her fine eye for color and her implied nod to an ancient architectural form. Artist that she was, she realized that the piece needed only minimal embellishment: The quilting is confined to the diamond shapes, and the finish is a narrow binding all around.

This large, spectacular quilt is a real treasure, a wonderful example of an American folk art.

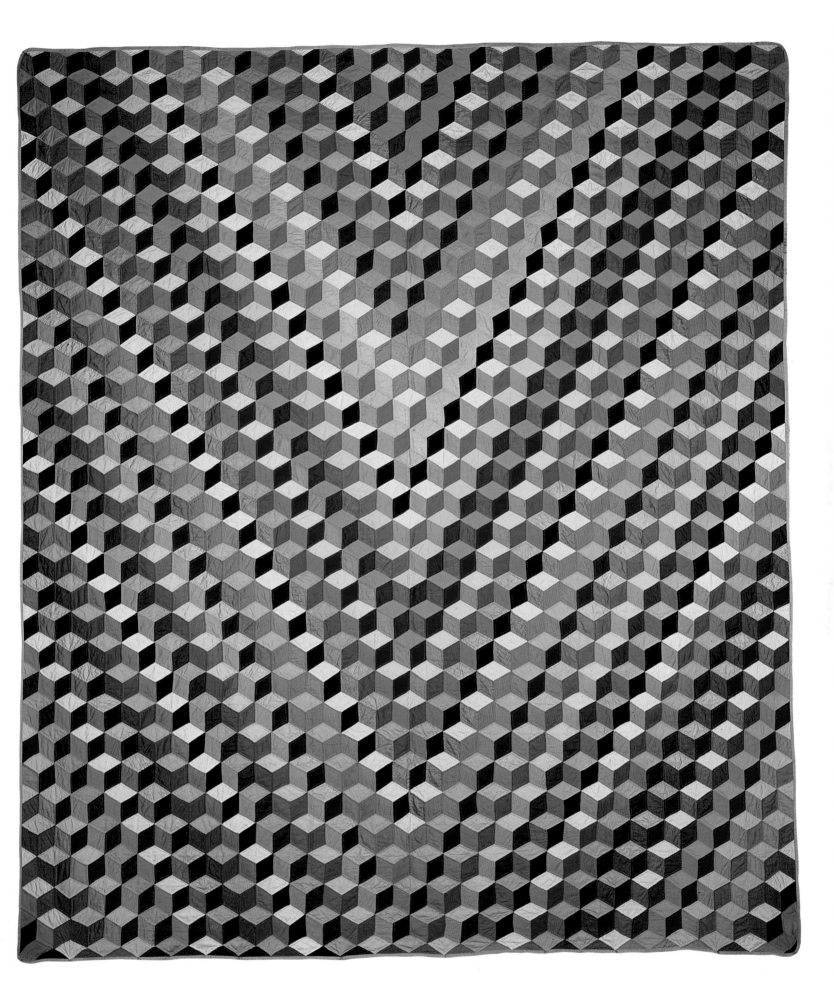

39

BROKEN DISHES
Pieced cotton. 81½×69″.
c. 1930. Midwest.
The Esprit Collection, San Francisco.

Midwestern Amish quilts, unlike their Pennsylvania cousins, were often made of cotton rather than wool. The designs, too, tended to follow more closely what we think of as the traditional patchwork patterns. The Broken Dishes pattern is a variation of the Pinwheel, or Windmill, pattern, in which two colors alternate within each eight-triangle motif. The Broken Dishes pattern, on the other hand, uses a different color for each of the eight triangles per block. Moreover, the motifs appear to be joined at random, so that light patches are scattered among dark, just as we might see in a heap of shattered plates. Among the colors used, there are several shades of pink that, in contrast to the darker colors of the other patches, really sparkle.

In the present example, two contrasting borders help to frame and unify the design. The narrow inner border is deep mauve, the wide outer one charcoal gray; both colors have already been used for some of the triangular patches in the center. The narrow binding around the edge matches the outer border. Each Broken Dish patch or triangle is quilted along all three inner edges with matching thread, creating a slight puffiness. For the inner border, the quilter has stitched a chain of pointed ovals, and for the outer border, a concentric series of overlapping scallops—again, with a slightly puffed effect.

40 FOUR-PATCH PIECED CRIB QUILT

Pieced cotton. 39×30″.
c. 1925. Holmes County, Ohio.
The Esprit Collection, San Francisco.

From its size, we can tell that this interesting quilt was intended for use in a baby's crib. The colors, however, are very far removed from the conventional nursery colors of today, whether soft pastels or bright primaries. These are definitely adult colors, scaled down to fit a very small bed. In fact, the quilt is a reflection, in miniature, of a color scheme commonly found in Holmes County quilts, with black playing an important role in setting off a bright pink and the more subdued blue, green, and several variations of brown. From this, we can infer that the Midwestern Amish treated their children—even babies—as miniature grown-ups.

The quilt's center panel is done in a pattern known as Jacob's Ladder, which is nothing more than a basic four-patch motif laid out diagonally, with triangles filling in the gaps. It is both charming and effective in its simplicity. A pieced Zigzag, or Streak-of-Lightning, border frames the center panel. In both of these areas of the quilt, the quilting stitches, which are fairly large, are easily visible. Whereas the triangles and pink border strips are outline-quilted, the small squares making up the four-patch blocks are more decoratively stitched with leaves, complete with center vein. The wide black outer border is quilted in a continuous-chain design. The quilt corners have been gently rounded off, and the edge is encased in contrasting binding.

41

JOSEPH'S COAT
Pieced cotton. 80×78".
c. 1890. Pennsylvania.
Collection America Hurrah Antiques, New York City.

In children's picture books of Bible stories, Joseph's "coat of many colors" is almost always depicted in bright multicolored stripes—very much like this glorious Mennonite quilt. The rainbow colors are repeated in a simple striped pattern to produce this richly hued and textured quilt. The diagonally striped border further enhances the sumptuous design.

There is nothing austere about this quilt, either in the use of color or in the amount of fabric needed to put it together. Unlike patchwork quilts—which in the early days, at least, were made from saved-up scraps and salvageable remnants of worn clothing—this Joseph's Coat quilt required considerable yardage of new fabric. Long strips of fabric were pieced together for the center section, and the pieced-strip fabric was cut on the bias to create the border. Whenever fabric is cut on the bias, there are always some unusable pieces left over. Therefore, some waste is unavoidable—a concept at odds with the usual pioneer practice of thrift.

Wasteful or not, most would agree that this quilt was worth a bit of extravagance. Contributing generously to the overall atmosphere of opulence is the puffy, almost three-dimensional quilting that covers virtually the entire piece. The red stripes are all stitched in a diamond pattern, and the other stripes are quilted with braided chains or plumes. Around the border are more plumes, and a plumed wreath sits in each corner.

42 PIECED STAR WITH SAWTOOTH BORDER

Pieced cotton. 85×88″.
c. 1890. Pennsylvania.
Courtesy Thos. K. Woodard American Antiques & Quilts, New York City.

More than 10,000 tiny pieces of fabric went into this marvel of a quilt, which comes from Pennsylvania and may be Mennonite in origin. Because of the extremely small size of the patches, this quilt could be classified as a Postage Stamp quilt, a term that refers to the size of the individual pieces, not to the size of the finished quilt.

Numerous calico prints, along with a few solids, are arranged and rearranged to form virtually unlimited combinations. Yet each small block contains the identical basic shapes needed to create an eight-pointed star: a center square, four smaller corner squares, eight tiny triangles, and four larger triangles. Depending on the way in which the colors and prints are placed, the relationships of the adjacent shapes vary, and the eye may perceive them differently. Thus, in some blocks, the star stands out unmistakably; in others, the star recedes and the center square advances. In still others, the visual impression is that of an X rather than a star. All of these different blocks are mixed together, by chance, into a star-spangled field.

The maker of the quilt chose a pale blue for the border, in which the star-block field seems to float. The border is actually a triple one, composed of two sets of blue strips separated by a sawtooth strip—another example of intricate piecing. The precise matching of the sawtooth triangles at the corners is an indication of the excellent needlework of the quilt's creator. Notable, too, is the slightly raised, ripple-patterned quilting along the borders.

43 RAY OF LIGHT

Jinny Beyer
Pieced cotton. 92×83″.
1982. Great Falls, Virginia.
Collection Good Housekeeping Magazine.

Jinny Beyer was, not surprisingly, a national winner in *Good Housekeeping* magazine's 1982 Great Quilt Contest with her breathtaking Ray of Light quilt. Though the colors and prints are subdued, they are deployed so artfully in conjunction with eggshell white that the entire work seems to glow.

The central compass, or starburst, motif sits within a diamond delineated by a sawtooth border; this, in turn, is framed by an elaborate square border containing sawtooth, diamond, and multiple-band elements. The piecing is precise and flawless. Smaller compass-within-a-diamond motifs surround the framed square, the intervening spaces being filled with triangles and diamonds in a Spanish-tile print. Working outward, an intermediate, multiband border of diamonds and triangles recalls the smaller version closer to the center. The pieced border immediately outside this one is skillfully constructed of triangular shapes and incorporates the recurring sawtooth motif. Once again, the positioning and the joining of the various elements are perfect.

Jinny Beyer's quilting virtuosity is evident as well. She has used several patterns to complement and accent the various areas and shapes of her quilt. For instance, in the center diamond-in-a-square, she has worked plumes and petals in the large white spaces and simpler outline quilting for the other shapes. On other areas of the quilt, she uses outline quilting again, along with parallel chevrons to highlight the white triangular shapes.

44 NAUTICAL STARS

Judy Mathieson
Pieced cotton. 88×73".
1987. Woodland Hills, California.
Collection the artist.

An anonymous sailor's watercolor on exhibit at the Green-field Village and Henry Ford Museum near Detroit, Michigan, was the inspiration for Judy Mathieson's star-studded quilt. As for the stars themselves, their heritage has such divergent sources as Pennsylvania Dutch hex signs and motifs on old quilts. The center decorations are the designer's own versions of the compass roses found on antique maps.

Dominating the design is the huge central star—or multiple stars, depending on how one looks at it. Together, the overlapping shapes and gentle gradation of colors create a vivid, whirling sense of movement, not unlike that of a ship's wheel. A large iridescent halo around the central star further intensifies the feeling of motion, with dozens of triangular elements all seeming to point clockwise. For the most part, the piecing was done by machine, with a few pieced and appliquéd details worked by hand.

The shaded background, with hand-quilted stitches radiating from the center, contributes greatly to the nautical atmosphere. The best way to appreciate fully this sea-and-sky ambience is to let the eye wander slowly around the edge of the quilt, thereby traveling from darkest night through dawn and sunrise to dusk and sunset . . . and finally back to night again. It is a lovely image, beautifully realized—and in this magical sky, the stars are always shining.

45 Rhythm/Color: Spanish Dance

Michael James
Pieced cotton and silk. 100×100″.
1985. Somerset Village, Massachusetts.
The Newark Museum, New Jersey.

In his series of quilts titled *Rhythm/Color*, Michael James, a leading contemporary artist, has taken the simple technique of strip piecing to the state-of-the-art level. In this example, subtitled *Spanish Dance*, the subtle gradation of colors from light to dark and the graceful curving shapes seem to sway like the dancers in Bizet's *Carmen*.

Using mostly solid colors and a few small prints, the artist assembled strips of fabric with precision and then cut them into a few basic geometric shapes—squares, triangles, sections of circles (arcs), and a few abstract curved arms—all on the diagonal. Then, always aware of the interplay of light and shadow, he joined the striped shapes to form large blocks. He set some of the shapes so that the stripes matched exactly at the seam lines, almost flowing into one another. The rest were turned 180 degrees to create a right-angle chevron where the stripes meet and, at the same time, a shift in movement.

In this quilt, there are four large blocks, virtually identical in terms of the shapes used to form them; each has at its center a diagonally checkered square. In terms of color, light, and inner shapes, however, each block makes its own impact, while at the same time interacting with the adjoining blocks. Around the border, which is also diagonally striped, the light again seems to dim and flare alternately, carrying the eye with it through a series of flawlessly matched corners and chevrons. Olé!

46 Dayglow

Judith Larzelere
Pieced cotton. 78×72″.
1986. Dedham, Massachusetts.
Collection the artist.

During the early days of our country, thrift-conscious quilters saved every scrap of fabric. Even the seemingly useless long, thin strips called strings were sewn together into quilts. Though obviously no longer concerned with economy, Judith Larzelere has created a radiant Dayglow quilt that can be considered a contemporary counterpart of early string quilts.

Using plain and polished cotton fabrics in the softest pastels, the artist has joined together hundreds of small pieces to form strips of varying colorations. The tiny crosswise bands give the strips a bamboo-like quality that, once the strips are all assembled, contributes a refreshing airiness to the entire piece. A few veins of tender spring green delineate the major areas of the design and establish the direction in which the strips are to run. Because the colors are so subtle, the merging of the various areas is, in many cases, almost imperceptible. Only by observing the shift in angles and the position of the green veins can one see the transition. Although each segment of the design embodies its own abstract pattern and makes its own visual impact, the quilt should also be viewed as a whole and enjoyed for its gentle wash of color and expert execution.

Significantly, this quilt was assembled and quilted by machine, the technology matching the contemporary spirit of the design. It was awarded a second prize at the Vermont Quilt Festival in 1986.

47

CONVERGING VALUES
Ramona Chinn
Pieced cotton. 29×29½".
1986. Anchorage, Alaska.
Collection the artist.

As this small masterpiece demonstrates, the use of the simplest of geometric shapes along with the knowledgeable placement of colors can result in a beautiful work of art. Ramona Chinn is a self-taught quilter who began developing her technique in 1974. The successful evolution of her craft is indisputable in this example of her work.

Using squares and rectangles of various widths, the quilt maker laid out her colors so that their values gradually deepen from top to bottom. Because the gradations are not uniform across the quilt, a distinct sensation of flow and movement develops. Viewing the quilt from bottom to top produces the illusion of emerging from deep shadow into a burst of sunlight, of night turning gradually into day. The theme of dark into light is maintained even in the binding around the edges: It is black around the dark portions of the quilt and lavender next to the lighter colors.

Although the focus is on the design, with its play of color and light, Ramona Chinn has added touches of hand quilting that enhance the entire work in an unobtrusive way. Each individual block has a diagonal row of stitches that stops short of the corners. The quilting gives a bit of dimension and puffiness to the work that is quite pleasing. And since the shapes of the blocks vary, the angles of the stitching vary, too, adding subtly to the overall sense of movement.

48 TUXEDO JUNCTION

Charlotte Patera
Pieced and reverse-appliquéd cotton. 72×72″.
1986. Noreto, California.
Collection the artist.

This dramatic quilt is one of a series of nine by which the artist, Charlotte Patera, pays homage to the music of Glenn Miller, the popular big-band leader of the 1930s and 1940s. The title *Tuxedo Junction*, one of Miller's hits, is interpreted here in a most refreshing manner. The mere mention of the word *tuxedo* conjures up an image of smart black and white, something we see in abundance here. Waves of whirling lines (symbolic of couples dancing to Miller's swing, perhaps) lead the eye directly to the center, where intersecting quilted "highways," pieced together from brightly colored fabrics, form a junction. The very center is a pieced checkerboard repeating the hot pink and orange of the highways.

Creating a quilt such as this requires immense skill and patience. It involves not only collecting the appropriate fabrics but also designing, executing, and assembling all the elements. An intricate and painstaking technique, reverse appliqué requires two or more layers of fabric, which are first basted together, face up. The top layer is then carefully slit or cut away in a specific design to reveal the next layer underneath. The cut edges of the top layer are turned under and sewn in place to the next layer by hand with small, almost invisible stitches. Both the swirl-motif and ring-motif squares that form the main portion of the quilt were created in this manner. The swirls are given further emphasis by the quilting stitches, which echo their graceful curves. Note, too, the notched corners—yet another device that draws the eye toward the "tuxedo junction."

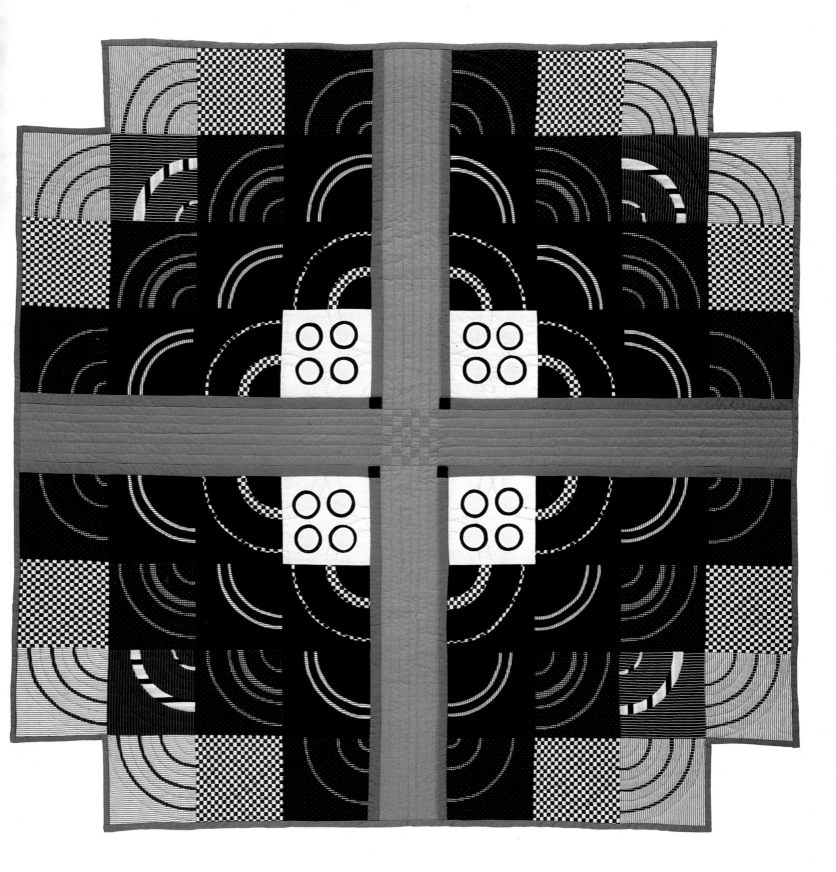

PHOTO CREDITS